MY

ITALIAN CATHOLIC

CHILDHOOD

Little Rosemarie of the 50's is Confessing Sins at the Gossip Window

BY ROSEMARIE CHAUVIN

WANDERING WORDS MEDIA

ISBN: **1717106056**
ISBN-13: **978-1717106056**

DEDICATION

I dedicate this book to several people in my life. First, my uncle, Dick. He would always ask me

"What's the story?"

My brother, Michael, I know you have helped me pen this tale from a spiritual realm. I love you! My entire dysfunctional "Pisano" family in heaven! "How's the beach house?"

My lifetime coauthor, silent conspirator, and partner, "Dusty." Thank you, Dusty, for being my sister. I couldn't imagine sharing our childhood drama with anyone else but you. You are the exemplary meaning of sisterhood in every facet. We are continuing our journey together. I love you, Mary Scalise!

My children, Paulette and Michelle Amaral. You are my blessings from above. I don't know what I did to deserve you as my children. You have made me proud to be your mother. We have weathered many hardships and heartaches together. We have kept one another sane, strong, and determined to push on in life. Failure is never an option. I love you to the ends of the earth, and pray that I didn't have to confess too many sins?

Last, but not least, by any means, my husband, Edward. Your unwavering support and confidence in me is deserving of a medal in itself. I thank you for rescuing me—from myself, at times. I couldn't ask for a more compassionate, caring, patient, and nonjudgmental partner. The additional gift of your melodic voice is a God-given treat. I love you!

Table of Contents

DEDICATION 4

DISCLAIMER: 10

PREFACE 12

Chapter 1 MY ITALIAN CATHOLIC FAMILY 20

Chapter 2 THOU SHALT NOT BRIBE JESUS 38

Chapter 3 THE DEVIL RUMOR 54

Chapter 4 THE SISTERS OF MERCY 70

Chapter 5 THE PALMER METHOD OF HANDWRITING 84

Chapter 6 SEX EDUCATION 98

Chapter 7 THE ACT OF CONTRITION 112

PRAYERS REFERENCED IN NARRATIVE 128

THE TEN COMMANDMENTS 128

ROSEMARIE'S COMMANDMENTS   **136**

ABOUT THE AUTHOR   **142**

ACKNOWLEDGMENTS   **145**

One Last Thing...   **147**

DISCLAIMER:

The prayers, commandments, and other religious recitations are from memory. Therefore, they may include error in presentation. There are no quotes or references from manuals, or specific Catholic prayer books, or other citations.

My intention with this narrative is for comic relief only. It by no means is an effort to make jest, or denigrate the Catholic faith or Italian heritage. It has been fun to have little Rosemarie share her experiences of the fifties era; from her childhood frame of reference. I am sure readers of this time period may especially appreciate this story.

PREFACE

Imagine you are a little girl growing up in the 1950s in a warped, Italian, Catholic family.

Well, I didn't have to imagine it. I had to *experience* it.

To be born into a strict, disciplined, Italian family, in itself was boggling. Add the Catholic religion, and the medley was a brew of confusion and discontent. Especially for a child with a sensitive, inquisitive personality.

That child was Little Rosemarie.

Even though Little Rosemarie of the 50s is now Adult Rosemarie of the 21st Century, many things remain true in her personality.

Adult Rosemarie needed to write this narrative based on the current times in comparison. She was musing over the past when Little Rosemarie poked her with a reminder.

The child reminded Adult Rosemarie of the how she would have enjoyed a more favorable childhood if she had been born in the current era. Children now are respected as individuals. The rigid conditions of the past have eased up. Little Rosemarie is in awe of the wide and varied changes of the times.

But Adult Rosemarie is still very much in touch with exactly how Little Rosemarie felt back then...

As Little Rosemarie trudges through her daily routine, she finds herself continually attempting to resolve and rationalize the conditions of her puzzling life. Her journey is more engaging and witty; divulged by the perceptions and rationalizations of youthful humor.

Old-fashioned family traditions, and the tutelage of the *Unmerciful Sisters of Mercy* left her no recourse but to make sure her voice and individuality were heard in one form or another.

There had to be a mistake. Heaven had to have played a trick. She was definitely misplaced in time.   Survival would not be easy for this sprite.

Life was unjust. She would fix it. The remedy was inside of her.

Children of the times were not allowed to assert themselves in a self-actualized manner. If they stood up for themselves or voiced an opinion, they were admonished. Admonished by family, the church, school, society, etc..

If the Unmerciful Sisters of Mercy were abusive to the children in class—why were they brides of Christ? Really? How come they never used the bathroom? Was it a perk of marriage to God?

These were all the questions Rosemarie needed answered. Who permitted them to guilt you into doing your work correctly? Everything was a sin against Jesus. You just had to look up at the cross suspended in front of the classroom to know that.

The answers to her questions were discussed by the adults at their congregational site: the "gossip window" where they gabbed about everyone. They made judgments at the window, resolved issues, and talked about the day.

The gossip window was the favorite form of entertainment, communication, and news. That and the stoop outside the house. Family and neighbors lived close by. Everyone knew everyone else's business and made a point of sharing.

"Hey, Johnnie! Gino had to go to the police station today. Know what he did this time?"

Rosemarie would persevere. Her fighting personality would shine through in one manner or another. She would make certain of that. Little Rosemarie would be heard. Her innocence and naive nature would take a stand against the insanity of the times.

Her struggles included dealing with three older siblings who chided her and squelched her voice. She resented their ability to place blame on her for things they did wrong.

The youngest child lacked the tools to defend herself. Sex education was a taboo topic, never to be discussed. Some knowledge of the topic would have helped; especially when she set the dinner table with the wrong type of napkins (I will let Little Rosemarie tell you *that* story herself!). Think of a young child trying so hard to justify, comprehend, and adapt to the times.

This culture was weird. The Catholic church, sin, confessing to a fallible priest—when Rosemarie could speak directly to Jesus or Mother Mary—was a waste of time. Of course, we would sin daily; wasn't that part of the process of growth?

The devil wasn't bad if he was serving your purpose. Neither was disagreeing with Jesus or asking Blessed Mother to do your bidding!

Little Rosemarie decided to make up her own commandments to live by; as well as her Bible.

There are so many of us who can relate and enjoy a good form of comical relief. Especially those who have had the same type of upbringing; be it Italian, Irish, Catholic,

Jewish, and all denominations of the times and culture.

That little girl still resides inside of Adult Rosemarie (okay okay—I admit, that's *me*).

She reminds me to keep living my truth, to stay strong, wise, and dignified. She implored me to share her experiences with you—the reader. She is proud of the adult that I have become. She has resolved and made peace with her childhood conditions.

Oh, and one more thing: Little Rosemarie is inviting you to come, sit, grab a drink. She is about to confess from the gossip window, so feel free to listen in....

Chapter 1

MY ITALIAN CATHOLIC FAMILY

The proof was scribed on my birth certificate. The defect was in plain sight. Dad relished naming me Rosaria—my mother's given title. She didn't favor that option, however. A petite version of a little Rosaria scampering around the house was negated. Instead, my name was compromised. I was dubbed two first names—Rose and Marie or Rosemarie. The defect? My parents haphazardly decided that I didn't require a middle name.

My original name was most likely considered a 'combo name.' Rose would be my birth name, and Marie would be my middle name. That was the assumed and unspoken message. There I was—signed, sealed, and delivered into the Italian Catholic family. "Look out world! Here I come!"

My family lacked insight into how not having a middle name would affect my necessary signatures as an adult. Future forms, documents, applications, and other paraphernalia glared deficit from the onset.

This change-of-life child—the fourth of three older siblings—was baptized by godparents who failed their initial test of guardianship on my behalf. Why didn't they question my parents about the slight? What baby gets christened without a middle name?

How many people can boast about having a middle name that is replaced by a zero, or a dash, or two question marks on the blank area next to 'fill in your full name?' My life was set up for failure!

Little Rosemarie would survive the fifties era! What a feat! Talk about "culture shock!"

In this period, offspring were to be obedient—as a given. That included listening, and doing as you were told; without questioning the reasons why.

"Because I told you so"—was the typical response. To deviate from the Italian Catholic tradition and customs would be viewed as a sin against God, your family, the church, school, society, and other unmentioned situations. Respect was fostered through fear and guilt. All under the guise or promise that someday we would be grateful for our impeccable upbringing. Then, and only then, would we realize the sacrifices they made for us.

My fraternal grandparents died long before I was born. I never got to make their acquaintance. My maternal grandfather, on the other hand, was a notable test of the times.

My maternal grandmother had passed when I was very young. The hushed-up rumor was that my grandfather had driven her crazy. God was merciful! That meant that he was kept on earth much longer. It enabled him to harass the remaining members of his family; his pawns.

There he stood. A short, stout, imposing, bald-headed man. The sight of him made me cower. He had the demeanor of a dictator. Unfortunately, visits were frequent; since he lived on the second floor of our two-storied home.

"Bouna Fortuna!"

My sister, Mary, and I jived when it came to Grandpa. An unspoken look at one another would render the giggles. We tried to stifle them by covering our hands over our mouths. We knew if Gramps saw that we were making fun of him, he would have a conniption. Anything could set him off.

Grandpa was a comical-looking character. He wore a white, sleeveless undershirt and baggy, blue pants held up by suspenders. That was the extent of his wardrobe. A protruding belly completed the ensemble. Speaking in his best

English dialect, he yelled "You makea funna mea?" The kitchen reeked of stifling pipe tobacco smoke. A spitoon rested next to his chair. Guess who always tripped over the spitty toon? Yours truly!

One of our chores, when we were visiting, was to make his bed. Straightening up the bed was a form of torture. "Get otta ter coma ova hier and sitta down!" The bed and mattress were so high, I felt as if I had shrunk two feet. Mary and I climbed on top of the bedding to straighten it out. The money bank was hidden between the mattress and boxspring, behind the cross positioned above the headboard, and inside picture frames. A goldmine. Anywhere where there was a crack or crevice was a viable place to hide the denaro.

Once seated at the table; he served us simple dishes like sliced tomatoes and onion salad drizzled with olive oil. Italian bread was always a staple. It tasted scrumptious dipped into any dish. Sopping up and absorbing all the juices of the meal with the crusty bread was pleasing to the palate. The aroma of the onions he served in this meal, though, could kill anything living and breathing. The scent was so strong that singeing the inside of one's nose hairs was a good probability.

Food was available for grazing at all times of the day. Breakfast, lunch, and dinner merged into an all-day buffet.

"Mangia! Mangia!" The thunderous voice vibrated the circumference of the kitchen. I glanced over at the china closet; the glass panes were still intact. One day, they would eventually succumb to the vibration of his tone. The delicate porcelain plates inside would become vulnerable to exposure and descent.

He methodically removed juice-sized glassware to pour the vino. Serving wine to six and nine-year-old children was not a favorable gesture, to say the least. Here we go again! Brace yourself! Another rant! Another fight about why children should not be drinking vino!

"They are too young, Pa!" My mother said wearily. He never understood that reasoning. Maybe in Italy, where he was born, they gave alcohol to children as a tradition. The tradition of giving wine to children in my family was unacceptable.

He scrutinized the refusal as a personal insult. Lack of respect was an attack on his integrity. He never seemed to understand the concept. Wine was a staple for him.

"Why you no drink? You no like?"

Was my grandfather setting up my sister and me to become future alcoholics? Maybe he was attempting to fortify our bodies. His intentions may have been medicinal. He wanted to build our tolerance to avoid future sickness and maladies. A method of consuming the non-consumable.

My aunt, Mary, (his daughter) seemed to have mastered the craft. She could drink with the best of them and never become inebriated. What really impressed me, however, was her ability to devour a medley of garlic, onion, and a ripped piece of Italian bread at the same time. She never flinched or feigned distaste. It was nothing for her to ravage hot peppers like popcorn. I was awestruck by her skill at mastering and consuming foods that were challenging to the palate.

Playing checkers or cards with Grandpa were two ways adopted to calm him down after the chaos and heated debates. "Thou shalt not disobey thy grandfather!" Confess it!

Four years later he passed away. Alone! Found on the bathroom floor, next to the toilet. The wake and funeral service seemed to stretch out for days. Mourning and tears. Wailing and drama! Visitors arrived and left; from morning to evening. They came in; they went out—like a revolving door.

The environment was so solemn for young children. No laughing or playing of any kind was allowed. It was a blatant sign of disrespect if anyone expressed happiness. That is, unless they were sharing pleasant memories of the deceased.

Stoic behavior was the order of the grieving period. A steady current of remorse, sorrow, and regret. I remember getting slapped by my mother for no apparent reason. People that came to pay their respects were strangers to me. Some were distant cousins; others were friends and acquaintances of the family from years ago. The only positive thing about the event was a constant flow of food, desserts, and Italian goodies. *Yum!*

Everyone was dressed in black. The women wore the color for at least three months to respect the deceased. High masses, candles, prayers, and rosaries were offered for the repose of the soul. I, myself, was confused by the sudden change in mindset of my mother and her siblings. "Pa" was transformed in death.

My mother's two sisters and three brothers always talked about what a bastard he was in life. Then miraculously, in death, he was a perfect father. It must be the guilt that follows death. Death and guilt have a deceitful manner of enabling you to see only the good characteristics of the departed.

Maybe the family thought they would be cursed if they talked negatively about grandpa.

Afterall, he could hear and see everything they were saying and doing. He could become even more powerful, and strike them from above if they spoke negatively about him in life.

My dad had a special book set aside for entries; used to write down the names of people who came to our family functions. Wakes, funerals, weddings, sacraments of Baptism, Communion, and Confirmation were documented in the journal. All notable occasions. It was used as a reference tool. A checklist to monitor those who attended the events, and what type of gift or monetary amount was offered. If we were sent an invitation from someone, the book would be perused to reciprocate and R.S.V.P.. No name on the list resulted in a negative outcome.

A conversation could go like this:

"That dirty bastard, the nerve! They never call! You never hear from them until they want you to attend their function. They can go to Hell! Don't respond to the invitation. They'll get the hint!"

Italian families were extended. Everyone in the neighborhood was related. They were considered your friends and neighbors as well.

Uncles, aunts, cousins, first, second, third, and twice removed all lived in the same vicinity. There were two-tenement and three-tenement houses to accommodate the gang. Next door, across the street, sideways and diagonally. They were spread in every direction, like an invasion.

Gossip was a hobby. It was rampant, tantalizing, and infectious. A delicious form of entertainment. It also served as a forum to opine and make positive or negative judgments about others. Conversations scanned a scope of topics from petty to severe. Nothing was off limits, with a few exceptions like sex; which will have a sole platform.

"Tony got a bloody nose at school today!"

"What? You calling me a liar? I'll punch your lights out! I told you the truth! Your son doesn't know how to fight. He deserved the punch in the nose! Come over here and say that to my face!"—Then came the silent treatment.

It could last for decades, or until someone died and then all would be ok with the family again. Apologies and tears would take center stage. The wonderful thing about having a substantial family was the unfailing loyalty. If a member was in a stressful situation due to finances, or illness, or loss; no one hesitated to assist in all forms. Cooking, cleaning, sitting with the children, running errands—any way they could lessen the burden and traumas of life. That was commendable!

The standard forms of entertainment were to sit on the stoop with a beverage in one hand and watch the neighborhood activity. The open window served as another. It was the more popular of the two. The window lends a bird's-eye view. Almost as good as watching the twelve-inch black and white TV with the adjustable antennae and two stations. Adjusting the rabbit ears could be a challenge to obtain the correct reception. The radio unit broadcasts music, variety shows, and a fifteen-minute soap opera titled, *The Edge of Night*. The telephone was a landline and numbers to make phone calls were dialed in manually.

"Hey, Luigi! Want some spaghetti and meatballs? Didja eat? How's your mother? Is she feeling any better?"

Children were always dressed appropriately for the weather. They played outdoors for all seasons in New England. Hopscotch, kick the can, jacks, jump rope, and tag to name a few. Winters were postcard perfect before the snow on the ground was disturbed by the hustle of the day. The blanket of winter wonderness hugged rooftops, trees, and sidewalks. Daytime invasions of delighted children sledding down hills, and crashing into mounds of snow and obstructed visuals.

Snowmen, snow forts, and snowball fights were imminent. Ice skating was a popular treat. Free fun for all to enjoy! Winters could be cutting. Many a time when clothes were hung on the clothesline, they were frozen to the line. The clothespins had to be pried away from the iced line. Towels and clothing were stiff and wet. Once taken indoors, the material had to be defrosted in front of the radiator.

We had to be home before dark when playing outside. If I was late getting home, I would hear my mother's voice beckoning. Rosem-a-r-i-e-eee! She didn't need a megaphone. Her roar echoed through the neighborhood. The *Marie* part of my defective name was accentuated. Unlike the romantic rendition of the name sung in the musical titled "Oh, Rosemarie, I Love You!" Nelson Eddy and Jeannette McDonald sang the harmonious score. She didn't have a voice like Kate Smith either; who sang on TV, "When The Moon Comes Over The Mountain—!"

Transportation was never an issue. Not everyone owned a vehicle. Food trucks delivered staples. Trucks roamed the streets. Vendors and peddlers announced their wares. "Get your fresh fish here!"

Apples, bananas, peaches, plums, grapes, and watermelon were chosen from the back of an open truck. The milkman delivered dairy; the breadman delivered breads and pastries. The meatman offered meats and cheese to the neighborhood. We even had a laundryman who picked up our dirty clothes once a week. He would return them clean, dried, and neatly folded. The favorite attention-getter of children was the ice cream man. Every day at three in the afternoon, he would ring his bell. Ding-a-ling! Ding-a-ling! The bell would summon kids to come running. They would connive for coins during the week to purchase an ice cream sandwich or dreamsicle. Doing extra chores around the home and helping neighbors was a way to earn extra money to buy the tempting treat.

We loved to eat! The salivary glands were always ready for consumption. A five-pound block of American cheese, salami, bologna, two sticks of pepperoni, and Italian bread were always available—just in case unexpected company came to visit. The guests would be enticed with a bountiful sandwich of meats and cheese topped off with sliced tomatoes, lettuce, and a healthy portion of olive oil. Who would be disappointed with that?

It didn't matter if you were prepared for impending visitors; an unkempt home could be remedied. We would stuff dirty dishes and silverware into the oven. As long as the pilot light wasn't lit in the back of the oven, everything was good to go. A match was used to ignite it when cooking and baking. Often, it took several attempts to keep the flame from fizzling. Any breeze would snuff it out. We would set the oven dial to the "off" position. Dishes and tableware baking in the oven would be a disastrous and embarrassing situation, to say the least.

A set of clean, white sheets was reserved for use as a table cover. There was also a set of special plates without cracks, and drinking cups unstained from the consumption of coffee or tea. The silverware was polished to a mirror image. Serving sets for twelve were counted and completed.

Since there were always children around; adults spoke in Italian, and sometimes a blend of both English and Italian. They didn't want us to figure out what they were saying; especially if they were speaking negatively about someone. Most of the time, in their haste, they swore in half and half. Half in English and half in Italian. At some point, the children figured out which were the dirty or bad words in each dialect.

Visits seemed to last forever. Every subject imaginable was discussed. Sometimes I wondered if they ever stopped talking long enough to swallow. Their mouths were continually moving. They ate, they talked, they laughed, they ate, they cried, they ate, they argued, they ate. Eventually, assuming they resolved the issues of the week; they departed. Remnants of the discussions remained. Soiled napkins, crumbs of bread, coffee and wine stains, and damaged tablecloths. Time to soak out the stains or purchase another set of sheets. Hopefully, a prolonged soaking in bleach-water would restore them to the original form.

My favorite part of the week was Sunday. I enjoyed family gatherings. Everyone would make a meal. Platters of antipasto, lasagna, meatballs and sausage, pizza and pastry. A traditional feast that could feed the entire population! Tables were placed together amicably. Chink! Chink! The glasses touched. Time to dig into the food. Time for young Rosemarie to open the window. She is beckoning you to sit, relax, and sip a beverage. "Subito! Hurry! The narrative is about to commence. Rosemarie is attempting to bribe Jesus!"

Chapter 2

THOU SHALT NOT BRIBE JESUS!

The majestic statue of the Sacred Heart was prominently displayed on the parlor mantel. His outstretched arms were beckoning me to spill my sins. The sin I committed against Jesus on my Communion day, however, would be no match for all the other little venials.

The steps leading up to Communion day was a process of learning. Catechism instruction and confession were required achievements before the sacrament could be received. The rules of the Catholic church determined the age of reason to be six years old. A child then possessed the ability to differentiate between right and wrong.

The entire method of going to obligatory confession was a story in itself. Talk about trauma! The confessional stall (alias death chamber) was located in an inconspicuous area of the church. We were to kneel down in the church pews and reflect on the sins we would confess to the priest, as we awaited our turn in the confessional.

One by one, we slid down the row as confessors completed the duty of cleansing their soul before receiving communion. I took issue with the priest interceding for me with Jesus. If Jesus resided inside of me, why couldn't I just speak with Him privately? Why did I need an intermediator?

Forgiveness would be quicker, and I won't have to go through the pains of confession. The priest was fallible and sinned as well. Why not do a reverse confession? "I'll tell you my sins, Father, now you tell me yours!" Young Rosemarie never understood the ritual.

Once inside the confessional, I waited for the priest to slide the window screen. That was my cue to begin my confession. Making the sign of the cross, I recited, "Bless me, Father, for I have sinned—"

***

A sin was committed in thought, word, or deed. In thought, I wanted to choke my older, bossy sister. In word, I lied to my father. "No, Daddy, I did not lose my mittens!" In deed, I sat on my brother's eyeglasses. A mistake?! The priest would then absolve me from my sins by making the sign of the cross.

Then I was given a penance of prayer before exiting the church. "Say three *Our Father's* and three *Hail Mary's* and try not to sin again." Right! Of course, I was going to sin again—over and over again. It wasn't like my goal in life was to become a martyr or saint! I was a kid! Kids sin! Such is life! I enjoyed cursing my family in thought and whisper. I was a little immature and inexperienced yet to execute the full extent of the word or deed part without getting my ass kicked.

The first confession was as numbing an experience as sitting in a dentist chair waiting for a tooth extraction. I learned that there were two types of sin. Venial and Mortal. Venial sin was an offense against God like the little ones I had confessed. They were a lesser evil. Mortal sin was a violation of God's law resulting in a separation from Him. Murder would be a good example. Mortal sin would be my haunt. The guilt would plague me. It was my secret! A secret I had harbored since Communion day. One I could never share or confess! Yes, I committed a mortal sin!

I couldn't imagine how my family would react if they ever found out my transgression.

When we were caught swearing, there was a special bar of Octagon laundry soap on reserve. What would they do to me if I told them I was guilty of a mortal sin? That large rectangular, brown, bubbleless bar was a mouthful of distaste. A good deterrent to swearing. They could decide to submerge me in the tub, surrounded with brown-tinged water from an endless dousing with the bars. Just to cleanse my corrupt soul! The thought of becoming a wrinkled prune-child was a turn-off. My secret would not be revealed to my family. No way!

"Honor thy father and thy mother!" "Thou shalt not take the name of the Lord thy God in vain!" Confess it!

I was pumped! It was happening! This was no ordinary Sunday. It was the day I would receive the Eucharist! The sacrament of Communion. I was pure inside and out. I was prepared. I confessed! I fasted! The usual breakfast of sunny side-up eggs with a splash of sauce was not allowed today. No Italian toast to dunk into the gooey concoction. I was even allowed to stroke my own ego and brag about becoming a child of Christ.

"Everyone keep away from me; I am holy! Don't get me dirty!" My mother had the tedious task of helping me dress in my white attire: Veil, dress, gloves, lacey socks, my favorite patterned leather shoes, white bag to hold my missal, rosary beads and embroidered hanky.

The procession into the church was remarkable. Boys dressed in white suits to the right and girls to the left of the church aisle. Miniature brides and grooms. The altar and pews were decorated with white flowers. The priest and altar boys awaited to greet us on this blessed occasion. Our parents and relatives nodded approval and smiled as we made our way to the reserved pews. *Alleluiah! Alleluiah!*

The priest talked to us about the sacrament we were about to receive. The body and blood of Christ. The gospel and sermon felt never-ending. Butterflies were dancing in my belly.

Communion time! This was it! I reached the altar-kneeler with my hands folded in prayer—waiting to receive the Holy Eucharist! My elbows gripped the railing as I swayed to keep my body in balance. I watched the other children receive the host. I was next! The priest placed the host on my tongue.

Then it happened! The sin! I panicked and chewed the Eucharist! In theory, I committed a sin. I murdered Jesus. I destroyed Him. I felt nauseated and embarrassed. Poor nieve Rosemarie. "Thou shalt not murder Jesus, in theory!" Confess it!

I had to put my shame and guilt to rest temporarily. We were having a party at my home, and it was time to partake in some good eats with family and friends. My parents even surprised me with a cake that said "Congratulations on your Communion, Rosemarie."

The name was squished onto the cake, of course, being too long and all. The defect! In my mind it read:

"Shame on you, Rosemarie. You consumed your maker!" Confess it!

***

I received religious gifts of rosary beads, prayer books, scapulars, crosses, and money. I never held so many green bills at one time. I was used to scrounging change for the ice cream man after all! I was gleefully counting my treasure when my nosy uncle squelched my elation.

"What you are doing is greedy! Counting to see how much money you have!" "Thou shalt not worship money!" Confess it!

I wanted to slap him for putting a damper on my special day. He had also interrupted my fleeting love affair with money. Didn't I have enough to worry about already with murdering my Savior and all? Now I had to add greed to the mix? I could only handle one crisis at a time. Murder took precedence over greed. After the celebration was concluded, I had to get back to the guilt-knocking shameful sin I had committed. A grave, mortal sin!

It didn't help any that my Communion picture was placed next to the Sacred Heart statue. How could I make amends to Jesus and save my soul? I certainly couldn't try to justify my actions to Blessed Mother. Jesus was her child. She may never forgive or protect me again. I finally found a solution to get back in God's good graces. I would make the ultimate sacrifice. I would give Him an offering He could not refuse. I had to think of something near and dear to me that I could present to Him. Just the thought of the gossip group discovering my secret would be unbearable.

"Hey, Katerina! Open the window! Did you hear what little Rosemarie did? She chewed the Eucharist at her first communion. Yep! You heard right! A mortal sin! Shame! Shame!"

My dad and I would take a trek to the candy shop once a week. I was allowed to choose the treat I desired. It was always a quarter-pound bag of confection that I didn't have to share with anyone else. I always preferred the round, black-button licorice; it was my favorite. I liked them so much! I would never entertain the thought of relinquishing one button. I was definitely not giving *them* up for Lent.

One piece of candy remained in the mouth forever—eventually shrinking into a thin round sliver of its original form. Jesus had to love the licorice too! I would give some to Jesus. I unclenched the endearing small white bag of candy from my chest.

The statue had two areas for candles. One candle holder was on the bottom right of the statue. The other candle holder was on the bottom left of the statue. We would light the candles when we were offering a prayer request to Jesus. I removed the candles and replaced them with my licorice buttons. "Jesus, please take my candies to Heaven and eat them. I am sorry for chewing your body and blood—you know, in the host, at my Communion. It is my most favorite, favorite candy! Enjoy and forgive me! Amen!"

***

My bribe worked. The very next day the licorice disappeared. I continued to sacrifice my candy weekly, without fail. Jesus ascended them into Heaven. How important was I? And He forgave me to boot! I breathed a huge sigh of relief. Release from the guilt of murdering Jesus was so gratifying. My secret was safe. God wasn't about to disclose it for sure. I didn't even have to confess it to the fallible priest, that was a plus in itself. He would have rushed out of the confessional; grabbing me by the arm while scolding me.

"You are no longer allowed to receive the Eucharist. This is a house of God. Heathens are not welcome here! We need to form an exorcism on you! You are an evil spawn of the devil!"

I didn't have to worry about any of that! Jesus was my pal! What a cool dude. I was sitting smug and satisfied with myself. Jesus liked my licorice too. I nailed that call.

That is until the unthinkable occurred! I couldn't believe my eyes. I caught my sister, Mary, sneaking and tiptoeing up to the statue to remove my licorice offering! I was aghast. I couldn't speak. I watched my sister take both licorice and proceed to pop one into her mouth! The unmediated nerve of her to steal from my Savior and me! As if that sinful behavior wasn't bad enough; she proceeded to skip and hum as she disappeared into her room.

As soon as I recovered from the shock of the scene, I confronted her.

"Why are you eating my Jesus candy? That is for Him! A sacrifice! I am telling Ma that you are a thief!" My faith was shattered. Jesus rejected me because my sister stole the candy before He took notice. She didn't deny that she performed the misdeed. As a matter of fact, she laughed and called me dumb.

"Do you really think Jesus wants anything from you? They don't eat in Heaven! He is too busy to bother with a pest like you!" She stomped off, laughing. I was so angry. *Oh, shit!* I thought. *Now what am I going to do?*

I ran and squealed to my parents.

"Mary took my candy from the statue and ate it! Give her a good beating!" My mother couldn't comprehend why I would put candy in the holders. She grinned. My sister informed her of what I doing with my candy. My mother said, "It is ok! You shared with your sister. So what? That was nice of you. Now go put the candles back in the holders!"

What the hell was it with older siblings anyway? I was always wrong. The older kids were always right. You were too little to bring anything substantial to the conversation. Too immature. I couldn't wait until I was old enough to tell them all what I thought of their demeaning treatment of the youngest child. I wanted to get revenge and make them feel shunned; as I felt. I stomped off to the bedroom and beat up my sister's dolls. That was a good start!

Dad was my comforter. After all, I was the baby of the family. He could make me laugh and feel better.

"Come on! Let's get a cookie!" he would say. This was his last opportunity to enjoy and spoil one of his children. That child was me. Besides, food was the healer of all ills.

As far as renewing my friendship with Jesus; I finally found a rationalized solution to my issue. I had no recourse. I had run out of options. My problem was solved because I decided I was not responsible for my sinful behavior. I was not to blame.

It was the fault of that slithering snake. The sneaky, sinister entity that wanted to inhabit my soul. The devil. The demon who tempted me on my Communion. What a revelation. He was jealous that I was one of God's children and he was not. He was cast into Hell. I don't know why he chose me out of all the other communicants. Must have been because I was purer of heart than the others. What gall! He was angry and made me chew the Eucharist. I had no control over the situation. What a creep! He tainted my holy day!

"Jesus, did you hear that? I'm absolved!" I couldn't wait to tell Blessed Mother that I was not responsible for the murder and that I needed her to use her sword of protection to battle evil. "Hail Mary! Hurry! Do you know what happened to me? Tell your son, ok?"

What a good little Catholic girl I had become. I must have been special since the mean devil wanted to possess me. He was my enemy. However, once I had finished patting myself on the back for my uniqueness—the fear set in! This devil thing was a bad omen. I was scared speechless!

I also learned that bribing Jesus was frowned upon. It was not a definition of theology in the realm of the Catholic church. Jesus was really watching me now; I had drawn His attention as well! Good or bad; I was viewed by those above and below in a negative light. "Thou shalt not bribe Jesus!" Licorice anyone? Confess it!

Another trial I had to grapple with was the devil rumor. My fear was about to implode.

Chapter 3

THE DEVIL RUMOR

The devil was an instigator! The initiator of wrongdoing and keeper of Hell! He was the reason one broke the Ten Commandments. A master craftsman of evil. I knew he was ever present. Opportunities arose in my daily life whereby I had to make choices between good and evil. I chose evil when the circumstance fit my version of the incident.

If I broke a glass or spilled milk, I would lie when asked who did it.

"I don't know! I've been in my room this whole time! The glass probably slipped off the table and broke itself!" "Thou shalt not befriend a demon!" Confess it!

The devil rumors left you even more susceptible to his wiles. The older Catholic children fabricated a dare that quickly spread among the younger siblings.

"I dare you to look in the mirror and say the name Satan three times. If you call him, he will hear you and absorb you through your reflection into Hell!" I concocted a scenario in my mind of how the dare would play out: A red devil with pointy horns and an elongated, twisted tail would appear in the mirror. Laughing, he would announce that he now had my soul, and I belonged to him for eternity. My appearance would convert into a miniature version of him. Goodbye, Rosemarie with the crooked bangs and missing top teeth. The curse could not be reversed! I would never see my original self again.

I realized my family was dysfunctional, but living with the devil was not my forte. Besides, how would my family recognize me? My mother would chase me around the kitchen with a broom, swatting at me, and yelling, "Get atta here! You are an unwelcome evil in this house! Shoo!"

Then I'd have no choice but to poke my dad's ankles with my pitchfork—begging him to rescue me. He'd want proof.

"Daddy, it's me! Here, have a licorice!"

Occasionally, I entertained the thought of putting the dare to the test, but quickly dismissed the falsehood.

***

Another rumor was the devil sabotage. If the devil decided that you were trying too hard to be good and getting too close to God, your soul was in jeopardy. You would draw remarkable attention and become ripe fruit for picking. A servile minion hovered above your bed; scrolling a checklist. His menial job was to mark off areas where you chose good over evil. Once he caught the "perfect" child, he could place you in a hypnotic dream state. He'd snicker as he slid your limp body to the foot of the bed and swiftly dragged it to the doldrums of Hell. Talk about a rude awakening! A revelation!

I hugged my rosary beads firmly to my chest and prayed to Blessed Mother and Jesus, "Lead me not into temptation! Deliver me from evil! Amen! Hail Mary! Hail Mary! Hail Mary!"—the shortcut prayer I used in emergency situations.

Devil mania ran in my family like a disease of sorts. I analyzed the familial situation. Everyone was suspect!

I had questionable proof. Devil possession may have influenced my brother, Michael, for example. He was encouraged by the devil to scare my cousin. Each time he babysat my cousin, he would wrap himself in ace bandages. Openings were left like slits for his eyes to view his victim.

Disguised as the mummy, he'd hide in the bedroom closet. Once my cousin fell asleep, he'd open the door, poke him awake, and scare him. After several incidents of bed-wetting and episodic nightmares, the cause of his fear was uncovered.

The mystery was solved. My cousin had never wet the bed or had experienced nightmares before the babysitting began. My brother was reprimanded and lost his babysitting privileges. He enjoyed every second of his nasty deeds. He was in no way remorseful for his behavior. He enjoyed scaring my cousin immensely. It reinforced his adeptness at disguise. He laughed and shared his skill with his devilish counterparts. The older siblings loved to tease and chide the younger ones.

I think a demon family possessed my great uncle, John, as well. He was a mean, crass person. He was my grandfather's brother. Figures. He never married and dismissed children as irritants. He didn't realize I was looking out the kitchen window when he decided to thoughtlessly behead a chicken in our backyard. The headless chicken ran around the yard clucking with blood spewing everywhere! Thank God I was spared seeing him chop the head off. I was traumatized! I freaked out! I screamed and yelled!

"Mommy! Uncle John—he killed a chicken!"

Well, he heard me! He looked up at the window. Mister Kind and Gentle ran up the stairs into my house and told my mother, "Shut that kid the fuck up!" In English!

"Thou shalt not treat children like garbage!" Confess it!

He was a heartless man to the core. Thank God he never married. God bless the woman who never became his spouse.

The devil played a part in my sister, Mary, and me getting into trouble as well. Most of the time, my sister and I did play together in spite of the age difference. She never told her friends that she enjoyed playing dolls and house with her younger sister. We played paper dolls and dress-up. We took turns playing 'family.'

"Let's pretend like you are the mom, and I am the dad, ok? Pretend like we are married and, uh, you are visiting with your kids, ok? You have ten kids! That's a lot!"

Our twin beds became tented homes with sheets tied to bedposts.

The symbols of protection were the traditional necklace of Italian families. The cross, the malocchio, and the Italian horn. The horn was a twisted amulet. The malocchio was a hand gesture to ward off bad luck and evil. We tied garlic together and hung it in the home on a string, next to the door. The stench would turn even the baddest of the bad away.

We anticipated good health and fortune. Religious medals of Saints and the Virgin were pinned on underwear. Scapulas and strips of palm from Palm Sunday were placed under pillows and alongside crosses of Jesus above headboards. Unfortunately, none of the above protected Mary and me from our impaired family. They executed an unwavering, authoritarian, and self-righteous way of life. Apparently, the devil influenced my parents as well! My sister and I got into trouble for things we didn't even know we did wrong! Talk about displaced aggression!

Take the "dirty look"—it was a penetrating stare. It meant you were doomed to get yelled at and hit with the belt as soon as "I get my hands on you!"

"Huh? What did I do now?"

They never seemed to forget anything either. Every punishment you received was justified. In fact, they could enlighten you to every negative habit and disobedient action you executed from birth. There was nowhere to hide. Here comes Ma with the infamous broom separating the twin beds. She would sweep the broom under the bed—discovering our hiding place. Doomsday! I wondered if she *rode* that broom when we were sleeping. She could wield that thing like a pro. After that one incident, I renamed my sister Dusty. The dust under the bed had attached itself to her curly hair. Reasons for the look stemmed from repeating something negative they said about someone else, to discussing our private business.

"This stays in this house and don't repeat it!"

There was no such thing as arguing or defending yourself. You were automatically at fault.

"You listen when I tell you to do something!" was the non-explanation for everything. It covered all bases. Brief and to the point.

"Can I go out and play, Mommy?"

"No!"

"Why not?"

The more you objected and asked questions; the more severe the punishment. You were a nag. You were annoying and disruptive.

When we visited family or friends, the rules were to "Sit in the chair and don't move. Don't ask for a drink, or eat anything, unless it is placed in front of you. Keep your mouth shut and listen. Be polite. Remember your manners and say please and thank you!"

There you sat, stiff as a statue, wishing to return home from the agonizing visit.

How does a naive child with a sensitive personality survive this era? It was a difficult, challenging feat—to say the least.

A visitor who came to our home monthly was my dad's cousin; who was a priest. So much for being a humble servant of the Lord. His ego was as large as his narratives!

My mother was extremely proud to have a priest visit. It made her feel extra special and closer to God. She enjoyed his visits as much as she enjoyed watching Bishop Sheen on our TV.

The Bishop's eyes were piercing. They stared down at you from the TV set. *Wow!* His biblical messages sent shockwaves down my spine. He was emphatic, curt; a master of the Bible and the laws of God. He was a force to be reckoned with. My dad's cousin, the priest, on the other hand, was the total opposite personality of Bishop Sheen. He was a braggart. He rambled on about how the parishioners loved him and showered him with gifts. Talk about penance! We had to sit and listen to him for three hours at a time. It was the respectful thing to do, of course.

In fact, there was a five-gallon bottle of burgundy wine kept on reserve—just for him—to sip and drink. Sharp provolone cheese and crackers complemented the vino. We all expelled a collective sigh of relief when he finally departed. My parents' sigh was of devoted appreciation for the visit. The children's sigh was for eye-rolling relief! The self-aggrandizing was over until the next month.

The times we received a break from monthly visits was when he went on vacation. Usually to Florida or near the beaches. *Hummmmm!* "Thou shalt not ogle women in bathing suits at the seashore!" Confess it!

I, myself, fancied the jolly friar monks. They seemed more laid back and jovial. Maybe because they were good bakers of bread and ate well. In fact, we had friar cookie jars. Ten cookie jars for the Ten Commandments—of course! Each had a commandment scrolled across their chubby, brown robe. I was enamored with the one that said, "Thou shalt not steal!"

One can guess what was put in that jar—cookies of course. Another puzzling comprehension. When you reached into the jar to take a cookie; were you stealing? The smiling friar could be tricking you to sin. How could it be stealing if the cookies were already purchased? Someone had to buy them in the store. How about homemade cookies? That wouldn't be considered stealing! If you helped yourself to a cookie without permission; it was stealing without permission. Why did my brain analyze such situations? When the cookie jar was empty, was it because the Friar ate the cookies?

"Mom, I took a cookie!"

"You what? Did you ask my permission? Now you can't have any for a snack. You had your snack already!"

Read the belly. Confess it!

I continued to fail life's test. My existence was a trial. My aunt even tricked me. She had a candy dish that played music when you lifted the cover. The candy dish happened to serve as a music box as well. The round candy ball I retrieved in the clear wrapper wasn't worth the lecture I was given. Caught in the act. "Thou shalt not steal with or without permission!" Confess it!

The gossip group would be ranting at the window, "Hey, Dino! Rumor has it that little Rosemarie is unrecognizable. The devil got her. She is a miniature version of his red self. Yeah! Tail and all. The kid is running around with a bag of licorice in her hand. Don't know why that is!"

I was sure of one thing. I was eager to become a grown-up—so I could be a know-it-all. I could speak my mind, and have the skills to solve the problems and challenges of life.

I'm sure that the devil disliked messing with the adults in my family. He didn't want to be thought of as a failure. An effort that the demon may not be able to continue to win. He could have just been lucky when he tricked my brother and uncle into doing his bidding. The garlic had to be a huge turnoff, for one. I'm convinced he didn't have the stamina to continue toying with them in a meaningless fashion. There were plenty of other souls to research and possess. You have to draw the line somewhere. Once the devil conferred with his fellow demons below; a unanimous vote was decided. Leave this dysfunctional family alone and just tempt them with the basic daily machinations. Satan could have been repulsed by *them* as well; waving his pitchfork in a dismissive gesture.

That is the reason young children were placed in Catholic schools. No one duped the nuns. They were professional fighters for Jesus. They had the tools to combat evil and keep it at bay. That is where children would learn the skills of their parents' desire.

The nuns were no competition for the devil. They held all the religious ammunition at their disposal. The nuns were an army of devoted soldiers of Christ. They gave everyone a run for their money. No one could put anything over on them. They could visit Hell and douse the little demons with holy water—keeping them in line for eternity.

It was an eternity I experienced five days a week. Monday through Friday. The order of nuns that taught at my school was the *Sisters of Mercy*. There had to be a misspelling in that title for sure. *The Unmerciful Sisters* was a more appropriate name for this class of religious instructors. Lord have mercy! They were fearless, ready for battle, and relentless.

Welcome to Catholic school. "Thou shalt not disobey the nuns!" Confess it!

Chapter 4

THE SISTERS OF MERCY

The Sisters of Mercy wore a wedding band to signify their union and marriage to God and His teachings. The letters R.S.M. meant Religious Sisters of Mercy. They vowed love, chastity, and obedience as humble servants. This particular sect dressed in black attire. Their garments reached their ankles. Black veils and white habits or coifs covered their heads. A white bib-like frontal collar covered the upper section of their chests.

Little Rosemarie assumed they shaved their heads, because not one lock of hair was exposed. Jesus had long hair. Why couldn't they? God created man in His image and likeness. My sacred heart statue was much more attractive than the drab look of the sisters.

The only people I knew who wore black forever were the Italian families in mourning. Maybe the nuns were mourning because they competed as jealous brides of Christ. They were trying to outdo one another for His attention. Celebrate your marriage! Dress in white!

My personal experience with the sisters was minimal—until I started parochial school. Encounters were brief and had to do with the school-related activities of my siblings. Such as selling candy bars to earn money for various school and church functions.

All that was about to change. Nine years sentenced to Catholic school instruction was unavoidable. "Hail Mary! Hail Mary! Hail Mary! Amen!"

The consensus was unanimous! Private Catholic education was a positive, well-rounded education. It covered religion and intense, instructional skills. The devotion of the sisters could not be matched. They had more time to teach without the responsibilities of a spouse and growing family.

My siblings purposely hid the perils of attending school from me. They were threatened with having their favorite Elvis Presley records destroyed or other valuable possessions ransacked or confiscated. "We need to protect Rosemarie. She is the baby and is very sensitive. I don't want you to scare her by telling her bad stories about school!"

The baby wasn't enrolled in half-day kindergarten classes either. She was to stay home because she needed to be shielded as long as possible. The lack of preparation and socialization of the classroom environment contributed to my turmoil. I was about to become raw meat, devoured by wolves disguised as nuns!

Needless to say, the first day of first grade was traumatic! My mother had the gall to leave me in class, up close and personal with a nun? No way! This was bullshit!

"Let's find your desk. Look for your name, Rosemarie."

"No thanks! I don't like it here, and I am leaving!" Looking around the room; I saw forty-two obedient children sitting quietly in their seats; tracing their name with a pencil. I began to cry. "I want to go home! Mommie-e-e-e-!" Sister Unmerciful ignored my wailing. Suddenly, she issued a stern warning: "If you don't stop crying, I am going to take you to the cloakroom and hang you from the hook! You are wasting my teaching time! Disobedient children are not tolerated in my classroom! Stop acting like a baby!"

"Thou shalt not baby the baby!" Confess it!

Nice orientation. The cloakroom was like an alcove in the hallway. It was an area designed with rows of hooks to hang coats, sweaters, hats, and other apparel. Sister Mean did not physically hang me from the hook. At this age, however, threats were taken literally. She left me in the cloakroom for the remainder of the dreadful day, communing with boots, coats, and hats.

So much for a cordial introduction into first grade. This bambino was expected to automatically change into a mature mini adult student.

I could hear the jeers of the gossip gang at the window:

"Hey, Maria! Rosemarie got in trouble on her first day of school! Do you believe it? What a stupido! Maybe she was adopted!"

"Thou shalt honor the brides of Jesus!" Confess it!

The nuns were basically made from the same cloth. Excuse the pun. They all shared and executed strict discipline. Students spent most of their school day with their guardians. It only stood to reason that they had undisputed rights to yell, hit, punish, and guilt you to submission.

Translating into mental, physical, emotional, scholastic, and spiritual abuse.

Personalities ranged from mean, meaner, meanest, to strict, stricter, strictest—"because God expects nothing less than perfection!"

The classroom setup was plain and dull. Individual desks were bolted to aged wood floors. Desks were as unattractive as the rest of the room. Desktops were worn and scratched. Most of them were engraved with initials of former victims. Crosses carved with the letters J.M.J. beneath them had to be a cry for help!

"Jesus, Mary, and Joseph, have mercy! Save me, Holy Family! Amen! Amen!" There were no welcoming, cutesy signs, or decorative invites for new students. If it didn't apply to learning; it didn't belong in the classroom. That was the rule for instruction.

A huge blackboard with a box of yellow chalk and two erasers rested on the blackboard ledge. Two pointers shared a space next to the chalkboard. The exception was red correction pens. There seemed to be a bountiful supply on the teacher's desk. The abundance of pens overflowed the pencil holder. Red pens to correct papers, assignments, homework, and tests.

Suspended from the cross, directly in the center of the room, above the blackboard, was the relic of Jesus. Each time I looked at the cross; I bowed my head in shame and sorrow—warranted or not.

The unmerciful sisters used the cross as a way of guilting you into submission. Guilt for not going to the children's nine o'clock mass on Sunday—guilt for not doing your homework correctly—guilt for failing your class assignments and tests—guilt for not knowing the answers to questions. It carried over to your sloppy work and desk, report cards, and disobedient behavior. Guilt to infinity! "Thou shalt not exhibit any of the listed deviant behaviors and then some!" Confess it!

Students' supplies were as meager as the supplies of the nuns. Two number-two pencils, an eraser, a box of primary colored crayons, and a ruler. Sister borrowed your ruler to swat your hand or whack your knuckles. Such compassion was unmatched. Of course, their reasoning for abusing you was always justified.

Writing and math papers were rationed. You did not receive an extra paper unless your writing was illegible. If your math paper had holes or smudges from erasing addition and subtraction problems, you received another paper for a redo. After Christmas break, you were alloted fresh pencils and erasers. If the ruler was broken across your hand from repeated whacks; that was replaced, as well.

Subject books were passed down from prior years. That meant no drawing, scribbling, marking, or doodling inside or outside of the books. We wrote our names on book covers we made from brown grocery bags. The cover looked gross when stained with grease or scuffed from being kicked or slid across a dirty surface.

Uniforms were mandatory. White blouses and blue jumpers for girls. Girls' knee-socks were blue or black to match the blue uniform. Boys wore white shirts and blue pants.

Another mandatory rule was that children were to attend the nine o'clock mass on Sunday. They were to sing in the choir directed by the choirmaster and organist. If you had the gall not to attend children's mass; you had to have an excuse written by your parent. It better be a good one too.

"What happened to you? Why weren't you at mass? I thought I didn't see you. Your name is on my list with a question mark. Your purpose at mass is to sing and praise the Lord."—In Latin no less—comprehension problems with the language excluded. If you were absent from school for more than three days; you'd better have a doctor's excuse or a very good reason—like being on your deathbed. Although the nuns wouldn't hesitate to call your house and inquire about your absence.

You raised your hand if you were thirsty, needed to use the restroom, or felt ill. Most of the time you were refused the request because you were interrupting the valuable lessons of instruction. You had to wait until Sister was finished speaking. That meant training your bladder and sphincter muscles to function before class, after recess, or after lunch—on schedule.

I wished I was as lucky as the nuns. It seemed that now that they were married to God, they forgot how it felt to use the bathroom. In other words, I reasoned, that one of the perks of being married to God was the exemption from bathroom urges. They were automatically dissolved. I concluded that there was no way they could manage pulling up and pushing down all those layers of dress. Their garments were too long and cumbersome. Their rosary beads would hit the floor. What was under those layers of clothing? Did they even wear those ugly thigh-length, pink, elastic, granny panties? The toilets were pull-chained to boot. Another perk I noticed, was that they never sweat in the summer months. Black—in their case—repelled, rather than absorbed the heat.

Disobedience or downright stupidity in all subjects resulted in a stint in the corner. A dunce cap was worn by the offender. Chewing gum in class was another offense punishable by a corner visit. The gum was spread across the top of the nose of the accused.

The school day began with a roll call. Before instruction began, we recited prayers we learned in class. On our knees; we declared the acts of faith, hope, and love. If we mumbled or rambled our prayers, or sounded insincere; we would repeat them. Sometimes we repeated the prayers three times before our recitations were satisfactory.

Obviously, the first subject of the day was Religion. I enjoyed learning about Jesus and His teachings. I enjoyed the parables. The sisters portrayed God as *punishing* more than *forgiving*. Now I realized why the devil feared the sisters. They were too much competition even for him. They were relentless warriors for Christ. I was a witness to their behavior every school day.

I was grateful for that aspect. I knew that the devil would never bother me while I was at school. The nuns would slap or whack the little demons with pointers or rulers—chasing them back to Hell. The Holy water and slap-whacking would sizzle them into oblivion. They acquired the spiritual ammunition to ward off evil. Blessed Mother taught them well.

My frequent conversation with Blessed Mother went like this: "Blessed Mother, I am confused. Have you checked on your helpers—the nuns—lately? They can be mean. I don't understand it. I like that they are mean to the devil; but not us. Please tell Jesus what is going on, ok? I love you! I know you are busy! Check in with my parents too. They also need to straighten out! Thank you! Hail Mary! Hail Mary! Hail Mary! Amen!"

I loved English and learning to read. Math was the difficult subject for me. The nuns did their best to make sure you passed your subjects. They lived together in a convent and conferred with one another on issues in the classroom. All desired to be good instructors and stewards.

So often I heard the sister ask questions like, "Why aren't you good at Math? Your brother never had a problem! Your sister was so sweet. She never gave me any trouble."

Siblings, cousins, and relatives before you, were taught by the same sisters. They compared your academic skills and personalities with those of relatives who came before you. Individual capabilities were not considered. If your sibling was good in a particular area of study; you were expected to excel in the same area of study. "Thou shalt not treat all siblings the same!" Confess it!

Handwriting was a subject in itself. It would even try the patience of the sisters. Students feared that period of the day. The thought would make one shudder with fright. A chill would run down my spine every time we had to switch to handwriting. An automatic moan from the class would be expelled when Sister announced that it was time to practice writing.

"Fill your inkwells and take out your pens. We are about to continue our work on the method of handwriting or calligraphy titled, "The Palmer Method of Handwriting!"

Chapter 5

THE PALMER METHOD OF HANDWRITING

The Palmer Method of Handwriting was the demise of many students. Austin Palmer created the cursive method of penmanship. It was a unique and fancy style of calligraphic art. We were taught this skill in third grade. It is hard not to associate Palmer with the Sisters of Mercy. So much angst could have been avoided if the finger/wrist motion of writing was adopted.

Palmer favored a form using a shoulder/arm motion to achieve the desired outcome. Practice! Practice! Practice! We practiced over and over and over again. The only way to master the art was practice!!! The additional challenge was having to write with an ink pen dipped into an inkwell.

Talk about penance! Practice lessons were to form tight concentric circles drawn on lined paper. The circles reminded me of slinky toys. Linear lines were peaked and oblique in form like a tight, slanted accordion.

The sister would stand at the blackboard and demonstrate the skill; pushing up the black sleeve of her garment as she wrote. "Everyone look and watch how we form the shape of the circles and lines." Yellow chalk dusted the front of her black dress; dispersing a pattern of color.

There was nowhere to hide when she stomped down the aisles to view your work. That is when the ruler transformed into a weapon-knuckle-cracker. You were stuck in your seat—forced to suffer the consequences of unreplicated work. Sister had an uncanny way of stiffening her body to an upright position when she was upset.

"You call that penmanship? Look at my example on the board. Your work doesn't look anything like it! Here's another paper! Do it again! That is not using your God-given talent. A disappointment to Him!"

"Thou shalt not practice incorrect writing for Jesus!" Confess it!

The cursive alphabet was also displayed above the blackboard, demonstrating the proper form of upper and lower-case letters. Mastering the calligraphic writing style, in itself, was intimidating. The additional task of ink, pen, and inkwell, was an entire topic in itself. Too much ink would require the use of an ink blotter. Too little ink required additional dipping into the well. There were two students in class who most likely grew up to become artists or employ that vocation—the teachers' pets. They finished their work early; enabling them to pass out papers, erase the blackboard, and slap erasers clean. They were definitely going to be God's favorites. He would greet them in Heaven when the time came, introduce them to St. Peter, and grant them special favors. I wanted to slap their smug little faces and kick them in the rear! Gag me! "Thou shalt not be jealous or wish harm on thy classmates." Confess it!

Notes would be sent home if a student didn't acquire the skill after a designated period. That meant that little Rosemarie would be another topic of conversation at the gossip window.

"Hey, Mary! Little Rosemarie did not get a certificate in Palmer writing after all! The kid is not too bright! I feel so bad for her parents! Such an embarrassment! What can you do? They can't give her away!"

***

Math was a grating subject for me. Carrying numbers in addition and problem-solving was beyond my comprehension. I despised the lessons almost as much as writing. Reading, English, and Spelling were my accomplished subjects. My dad was a great speller. We would have spelling contests at home. He would pretend to misspell a word so that I would beat him. "Take that, gossip junkies!"

Another joyful event was weekly tests. Spelling tests and multiple choice questions offered an easy method of cheating.

"Psst! Turn your paper this way so I can copy it." No way was I helping anyone cheat. The thought made me jittery. I knew better. The nuns had eagle eyes. They didn't miss a trick. Their vision could fixate and encompass the entire room without them even turning their heads! Must have been another wedding gift from God. Of course, I am sure one of the little red devils tapped her with his pitchfork and whispered, "Sister, Sister, kids are cheating! Good devilish behavior! Go gett'em!"

My trained, scheduled bladder had tough retention when Sister Mean went into action. She could topple the desk over in one swoop, as her face turned to a crimson flush. I wanted to run out of that room, hands covering my ears yelling, "Hail Mary! Hail Mary! Hail Mary!"

"Get up! You're cheating! Not in this classroom! That is because you're too busy daydreaming and not listening when I am teaching! You are lazy and a disgrace! Go sit in the corner; I will deal with you later. As part of your homework assignment, you are to write this sentence fifty times. "I will not cheat in class! Jesus is heartbroken." Now for the rest of you; you have fifteen minutes to finish. Step on it!"

Eagle Eyes would then stand in front of the class; swinging her rosary beads from her waist; scoping out her next victim.

I had my own test-taking issues to overcome. The end-of-quarter tests were more intense. It was called 'cramming as much knowledge into your brain as possible.' As long as I passed the tests and skipped the ridicule and guilt associated with failing; I would be fine. Jesus was watching from the cross.

The cross was a constant reminder that God sees all. More pressure! A simple hypothesis and solution was never the case, however. The left and right side of my brain were not in sync when it came time to take tests. These cumulative exams determined your report card average and final grade. End-of-year promotion to the next blissful grade-level was determined by how well you did in your test subjects.

There I was with the test on my desk. "Fifty minutes. When the bell rings, stop writing and put your pencils down!" I'm telling my brain to give me the answers. It decides to go on strike or take a brief vacation.

"Nay! I'm doing a brain freeze panic. I don't like the way you crammed info into me. You know I will only retain it short-term. You are abusing my muscle. Forget it. I will defrost when there are fifteen minutes left to the test to fill your blank page. Hope you can complete your work before the ding-ding-ding of the bell-bell-bell!"

"Thou shalt not cram material into thy brain!" Confess it!

It happened every time without fail. It seemed that I couldn't do anything right. I had to go through demon-Hell to excel in my subjects and complete my tasks.

"See Me!" was written in red ink at the top of your paper with those pens that kept replicating themselves. If you flunked a test, Sister wrote those two ungodly words on your paper. Schoolwork, homework—any and all materials that were handed in to be graded. "See Me" after school so that I can reprimand you. "See Me," so I can give you a note to take home to your parents. "See Me," to stay after school. "See Me" for tutoring. "See Me," to have a conference with your parents. "See Me," if you are unable to keep up with classwork, and do the required assignments.

Staying after school didn't bother the nuns. They lived conveniently in the convent next door. The stress of living a family life did not apply to them. No husband, no children, and no family obligations were advantages for them. The lifestyle of the sisters was not advantageous to the student who was the recipient of the admonishment, however.

My father, believe it or not, managed to get into trouble with one of the sisters. An entire class was kept after school one Friday. They must have disobeyed Jesus big time. My brother, Michael, went to check on some of his friends, to see how much longer the torture would last. He opened the door and announced his presence by waving a loaf of Italian bread he had purchased to take home. The kids started to laugh.

Of course, Sister did not find the interruption humorous in the least. His gesture was quite disrespectful. Therefore, my dad was summoned to speak with the sister about my brother's behavior. Sending my dad to the conference was not a good choice. He began to laugh when Sister explained the issue.

Both my dad and brother got into trouble when they returned home. My mother was appalled at their disrespectful shenanigans. Laughing at a holy nun was not acceptable! They received the silent treatment—once she finished lecturing them. "Thou shalt not make fun of the nuns!" Confess it!

Report card distribution was a very serious occasion. It was reserved for a special nun.

Mother Superior was the principal of the school. She would glide into the classroom with a style of dignity and grace. She conducted herself as a movie star prepared to be photographed on the red carpet. Her voice was squeaky and strained. She was short and slender. Mother Superior visited every classroom to hand out report cards; beginning with first grade. How lucky can one be? For some weird reason, she held a pointer in her bony fingers—like a scepter—as she delivered her vocational speech.

"As future nuns and priests; I expect the best work from all of you. All grades count toward achievement of this goal!"

Did I hear her right? There was no way I was going to parade around in that getup. I hated wearing the ugly school uniforms, as it was. I planned to become a wife and mother with children and raise a family. I loved role-playing as a married adult, instead of role-playing as a nun. I knew God did not want me as one of His chosen nuns. I liked combing my hair. I refused that calling. "Bye!"

Mother Superior *acted* superior. She would stand in the center of the room and call our names in alphabetical order to receive our report cards. That is, after she scrutinized our grades. Everyone knew your status. A "tsk tsk" meant 'shame on you.' A smile meant 'good job.' A nod of her head meant 'mediocre work.'

A dirty look with a side-to-side head-turn meant 'no hope.' No hope of passing into the next grade. Perish the thought! A repeat performance of the same materials with the same sister. What a fate! Another year sentenced in Hell. Not me! There was no way I was repeating a grade in that school. Thank God I never had to be retained. Someone up there was guiding me.

The gossip window would perform a litany of rebuffs if I ever had to repeat a grade.

"Hey, Angie! Guess what? Rosemarie failed! Yep, that's right—failed! She is not going to pass into the next grade. What a dummy!"—as she made the sign of the cross and kissed the invisible cross. "She not only sinned against Jesus and Mary, but she disgraced her entire family. I hope they don't move because of it. They are such good people. We would miss them. They are our blood, after all. Could be, they dropped her on her head as an infant? Who knows? If they did, they kept a good secret. Public school is a good idea for her. Catholic school is just too hard for the poor little thing. Let's pray for the family. They do have a burden with this last child. Hail Mary, give them grace!"

I know one subject that the Almighty, know-it-all nuns, and Mother Superior were not superior and knowledgeable about: "Sex!" There was no way they could teach sex education. What experience did they have? That subject would be sure to stump them.

"Sister! Can you say it, spell it? Could you say the word sex in spelling bee form? What is the dictionary meaning? Can you use the word in a sentence? What? I can't hear you. Please don't run out of the room; I was just kidding! Hee!"

That subject would definitely warrant a school expulsion!

My dreams of getting married and having children were shattered by that dirty word. My sex education (or lack thereof I should say), curbed my future desire. Although I did not change my mind on becoming a nun; I decided to be single and celibate. My mind was made up, and there was no way I was about to change it. "Thou shalt not have dirty sex!" Confess it!

Chapter 6

SEX EDUCATION

The word "sex" was a taboo term stifling sex education. In fact, the learning process did not include using the two words together. Sex was never considered a lesson in education. How could you discuss a topic that was never allowed to be discussed? That instruction would never be considered in mind or practice. There was no viable way to discuss sex unless it was under dire circumstances.

The mere mention of that "dirty" word would elicit an automatic transformation of adult behavior. Devilish senses were peaked. All forms of motion were suspended. Eyebrows raised, eyes bulged, ears perked, mouths chattered: "Smells fishy. Tastes sinful." Remember the definition of venial sin. "Thou shalt not encourage sex in thought, word, or deed!" Cryptic! Confess it!

In fact, my maternal grandmother waited until my mother's wedding day to reveal important information about childbearing. My parents were engaged for four years. They wanted to wait for the depression era to pass before they were wed.

Finally, on the happiest and most celebratory (every girl's dream) wedding day; my grandmother relayed a secret.

"Rosaria, you have only one fallopian tube. You may not be able to have children."

"Whaaaaat?"

What a wonderful time to share that bit of encouraging news. The great depression; four years of engagement; and a joyful announcement on Mom's wedding day. Nothing like waiting for your child's special day to uncover the great reveal! To ask the how's and why's or details on the subject would be a fruitless attempt. Anything having to do with sex was not up for debate.

I don't know how my mother broke the good news to my dad on their honeymoon. "Hey Honey, guess what? We may not be able to conceive—just found out!" Nice gift! Nice mother-daughter words of wisdom and prenuptial advice!

After four years of marital bliss, my oldest brother was born. He was treated like a king—since he was an unexpected surprise! Three years later, another surprise was born; my second brother. Three years after that, the first girl was born. Three years later, came little Rosemarie; the last child of a barren mother? I was the grand prize baby. My mother conceived me when she was in her forties. The time of life when having children was diminished. Maybe the three-year cycle of our births was timed by the Holy Trinity. The

Father, Son, and Holy Spirit. Imagine if both her fallopian tubes were intact! I could have had a slew of younger siblings to boss around and tease.

Young Rosemarie's sex education was summed up in a brief, but poignant sentence: "Kiss a boy, and you will get pregnant!"

Amen! That meant, then, that my parents kissed *how many times* before each conception?

I made a point of staying away from boys after that orientation. When we played tag at the playground; I stood my ground and kept my distance. That is, until the fateful day a boy rushed up to me and planted a kiss smack on my mouth. I pushed him away.

"What did you do that for?" I panicked. I charged into the house in tears and stammered, "I'mmmm preg-a-nant! A boy kisse-e-ed me! He came out of nowhere! It was not my fault! Maaaaaa!"

I stared at my parents who were busy cooking. *So what else is new?* They didn't flinch or show concern. *What the hell was that all about?* My dad kept stirring the sauce on top of the stove. My mother kept rolling meatballs.

Dad's comment; "Hey Rosemarie! Want some pasta fagioli? I just put it in the bowl. I added your favorite beans!"

Jesus, Mary, and Joseph; what was their problem? I told them I was pregnant for goodness sake. React! Any feedback here? My father reached for a fried meatball, put it on a plate, and served it to me. That concluded the non-discussion. Ignore the subject! Keep eating! Food is the healer of all wounds! *Why am I the only one upset here? A fried meatball isn't going to fix my pregnancy!*

My mother finally chimed in, "You didn't do it on purpose. You didn't know the boy was going to kiss you. It was not your fault, so it doesn't count. You are not pregnant. Now eat your meatball! Want some sauce on it?"

What the heck did that mean? He still kissed me. My fault or not!

Then I reasoned with myself—*I got it!* Since I did not consent to the kiss, becoming pregnant automatically dissolved itself. How impressive was that? "Thou shalt not give thy kid the brushoff!" Confess it!

The day I did learn about "taboo" sex was not anticipated. There was no preparation; and my sister was the culprit. She had accomplices; my five female cousins. The day began innocently enough. I was over-the-top elated that my older sister and cousins invited me to dine with them. Why? I didn't care! I was just happy that they had included me in their grown-up conversations and activities. Maybe they took pity on me because I longed to be part of their group. An act of kindness or a sacrifice to God. Who knew? I could have been viewed as mature beyond my years, right? Therefore the invite.

My big girl job was to go upstairs, find the napkins, and set the table. Simple enough. I didn't even have to look into a cabinet. The huge box of napkins was conveniently located on the floor, in a corner, next to the bathroom. It was an odd area to store napkins. I shrugged it off, thinking someone forgot to put them in their proper place.

My immediate goal was to impress my family as an equivalent member; who cared why the napkins were misplaced? The box read: "Super absorbent Overnight Sanitary Napkins!" Wow! How unique! I removed one from the box. A new kind of napkin! They were extra sanitary and absorbent. I had never seen napkins so thick and oddly shaped. They could handle the job of messy olive oil and gravy spills. What a find! You only needed one napkin to wipe your face and swipe crumbs from the table. A much neater way to present your well-mannered self.

Each napkin had a front and back piece of thin material attached to them. I made a mental note of asking my cousins how the silverware was tied to the tabs. The important thing was that I set the table. The fork, knife, and spoon looked spiffy on top of the individual clouds of thickness—with or without the tabs.

I couldn't wait to show off my décor. The girls were busy serving up plates of food. They either forgot I was around or forgot to check on me. Bad mistake! My elation was short lived. My cousin almost dropped the platter of antipasto she was carrying to the table. My sister's mouth was agape. They all stared at my sister in disbelief. They also looked at me.

After the initial shock passed, one of them asked me, "Honey, do you know what we use those napkins for? They are not to wipe our mouths."

One of my cousins laughed and said, "Wrong end!"

Another said to me, "These napkins are for special occasions. Let's put them away, and we will discuss it after dessert."

Needless to say, dessert for me, was not a dish of spumoni! It was a crude, blunt, slap-in-the-face, lesson on the "facts of life"—Italian style.

In those days, Kotex, or sanitary napkins, were held in place by a sanitary belt. The tabs of the pad fit through openings in the front and back of the belt. The belt kept the pad in place.

My courageous sister and cousins decided it was time to talk to me about sex. Hopefully, to avoid any further embarrassing situations, as the above mentioned. *Oh my God!* The gossip gang would have had a good laugh on that one! Of course, it would have to be at the girl gossip window. We don't speak that kind of talk in front of men. Show some respect and decency for yourself!

"Hey, Vivian! This is the best one yet! They didn't tell little Rosemarie about Bloody Mary and her monthly visits. She thought Kotex were table napkins! Wipe your mouth on *that* piece of information." "Ha! Ha! My belly is hurting from laughing! Stop! You're shitting me right? Close the window! Shh! Here comes your husband!"

I finally became enlightened as to why sex was an evil word. I envisioned a young girl in a long, white dress, knocking at my door every month. I was compelled to open the door because she was my monthly companion. She would be standing there with blood trickling from her eyes and down her white nightgown.

That wasn't the end of it. I learned the reason women menstruated monthly. At one point, I couldn't take it anymore, and told them they were rotten for telling me such lies. Who makes this kind of stuff up? They all agreed that it was true. "Thou shalt not tell scary sex tales!" They all confessed it!!!!

My head was spinning with information that I didn't want to hear. Each additional fact lends a revolt in itself. If I told my mother—or anyone—about our conversation on sex, or who told me; I was dead. They would never admit it or talk to me again.

Intercourse! I couldn't even pronounce or begin to know the meaning of that word. The thought of a man and woman performing that act *had* to be a fallacy. There was no way God created sex. What was He thinking? "A man has a penis? And where does he put it? Are you for real?"

It must be detachable. When he wanted to make love and start a family, he could attach it back on like velcro. That had to be the only reason. Why else would he walk around with that bundle hanging in front of his body? Full exposure! They never told me that the sexual act was for pleasure. Girls didn't have anything you could see. You needed a mirror to see anything. Who wanted to anyway? "Wave, little monthly Mary! Raise your bloody hand!"

How could sex, an evil abomination, be a loving pleasure? A man and woman had to really love one another to perform the sexual act. I'm sure they could profess their love in another manner! Love-making was an extreme. Nobody was touching *my* body that way. Choose another profession, Rosemarie! "Thou Shalt Not Make Love to a Man!" Confess it!

The thought of my parents having done the deed—at least four times—made me nauseous! How could they stoop so low? I couldn't even look at them without feeling disapproval and disgust.

I told my sister to stay away from me. I had to sort this burden of information out for myself. First, I went to talk to the statue of the

Sacred Heart. "How could you invent such a disgusting thing, Jesus? Was it really you? Is it true? I am so disappointed in you. Forgive me! "Thou shalt not argue with thy Heavenly Father" Confess it!

Slowly, it all began to make sense. Now, I understood why so many Catholic children became nuns and priests. The nuns encouraged these vocations because of the sexual aspect to it. I was becoming enlightened. I had a long talk with Blessed Mother, as well.

"Blessed Mother, you know how much I love you. You are my favorite. I don't understand why your son, Jesus, created this sex stuff. It is not a good idea. I need a favor from you. I totally understand why the angel Gabriel came to you. You didn't get pregnant the "natural way"—good for you. Now I want you to do me a huge favor. When I grow up, and that is a long, long time from now—so write it down, ok? Not that you would forget—but please ask the angel Gabriel to visit me too; if I ever want kids. My husband will have to feel the same way. No sex! That is, if I do get married. Ok? Jesus hates to refuse His mother. He will do whatever you ask! Please! Please! Please! My beautiful Mother and thank you! Hail Mary! Hail Mary! Hail Mary!"

Now I would gain respect, adoration, and praise, from the gossip clan.

"Hey, Jean! Whoever thought that little Rosemarie; that little crybaby, eating Jesus at Communion; would become so famous. What did she do to get the angel Gabriel to give her kids by a miracle? They had to stop those monthly visits from Bloody Mary. She must be special! God Bless her! She was always such a good child. Never a complaint about her; nope. An angel on earth! The Immaculate Conception!"

Little Rosemarie was caught up in a web of confusion. There was no adult she could confide in to confirm, or deny, the revolting and traumatic discussion about sex. What information was factual? Which bits and pieces were lies, for embellishment sake? Was it all a joke to taunt her? It was all assumption! She was sure of one thing; she didn't like any part of S—E—X; true, untrue, or anywhere between.

As far as she was concerned, there was some contrition due on the part of her dysfunctional family! It would be in their best interests to recite the Act of Contrition. "Oh my God, I am heartily sorry!"—"Thou shalt admit thy dysfunctionality!" Confess it!

Chapter 7

THE ACT OF CONTRITION

Adult Rosemarie, minus a middle named birthright, lost the members of her dysfunctional fifties family. Nostalgic musings of the gossip clan reciting the "Act of Contrition" before entering Heaven is plausible.

In unison: "Oh, my God, I am heartily sorry for having offended Thee—."

The spokesman; my grandfather: "St. Peta, wadda we godda say a pray for? Eh? We a good familia and belonga in Heaven! You needa proof? Let me cooka for you! Makea room for us!"

Open the golden gates and clear the bridge. St. Peter had a meeting with the Apostles.

"Where do we put this group? Are they all staying in Heaven? Are some going down to Hell? Anybody doing a stint in Purgatory?" The consensus was to put them all at the beach house where they used to enjoy family gatherings. The devil weighed in on the situation. He didn't want any of them. He remembered this family when they were alive. He could have easily shuttled them to Hell, but he reneged on the idea. This group was even too hot for Hell! "Pass the vino."

The Sacred Heart of Jesus statue is also a memory. However, I'd like to take some credit for murdering Jesus, in theory. The host can be chewed. Maybe Jesus heard my guilt-ridden apologies after all—licorice bribe or not. "Mea Cupa!"

God took away the special bathroom privileges of the nuns, who can currently wear civilian attire. It's only fair. They also have locks that can be combed and styled. Talk about a change! A cross worn around their neck signifies they are a religious order. I was tricked by them several times. A lot of people wear crosses. So I didn't grasp the distinction that they were nuns. A conversation with your peers may go like this " . . . then that dumb, stupid bastard—"

"Hello! I'm Sister—" A nun comes quietly sauntering to the group. They still have that sneaky "gotcha!" demeanor.

Flashback! Gulp! "Hail Mary! Hail Mary! Hail Mary! Amen!"

Although their attire may have changed to match the era, they still have no experience in sex education. Okay sure, they are more knowledgeable—yes—but they can't practice what they preach! *Hum!*

Speaking of practice, "The Palmer Method of Handwriting" was brutal. All those red-knuckled hands to what avail? My penmanship is horrible. Much like a prescription written in scribble by a doctor. At times, I can't even decipher my hurried shopping list. How bad is that? Maybe my inner-child is still rebelling against the calligraphic form of cursive script.

I often think of the other kids in class; of course, including the two teacher's pets. I wonder if the pets became artists—or members of a religious order. I think about my fellow classmates sometimes; were those knuckle-wacking beatings worth the effort? Did they eventually excel in handwriting—or are they members of the scribble club? I have indelible mental scars from the experience.

The current era's children are treated as individuals with expressive egos. Thank God for that. They have a voice, and they use it! I have had the honor and privilege of working with the kindergarten children for fourteen years. They keep you young at heart, and tickle your inner-child with their spirited personalities.

The classroom environment has drastically improved. Children are greeted with strategically placed welcome signs. Classroom halls and doors are colorfully decorated with names of classmates and teachers.

Fun packets of supplies for school and home are displayed. Brief greetings and parent/teacher questions and issues are addressed during meet and greet events. Bulletin boards are festively decorated in colored paper; with subject headings at the center of each board. There are ample centers in the classroom, for all subjects.

There are book libraries, designated areas for math and manipulatives, writing, and computers. Amenities such as a media center, computer lab, physical education, music classes, and a cafeteria are standard. Supplies are unlimited and fun. Markers, colored pencils, crayons of every hue, math manipulatives, and puzzles—to name a few. The environment is pleasant and engaging.

Every opportunity for learning and challenges are encouraged.

Field trips are planned to science observatories and theme parks. Career days at school are invites for professionals; to share their knowledge, and tout their vocation. Be it dentist, or scuba diver, or chef. No, the priesthood and convent are not discussed as vocations, just saying...

Dusty and I also changed the flavor of religious education. We taught CCD religious classes to kindergarten and first-graders. We learned more about Jesus as loving and forgiving. There was no way we were going to invite the devil into the conversation, or impose guilt on the children. We all sin—because we are not perfect beings. Besides; I finally took a stance with the devil and told him to "Stay in Hell! Eat some licorice!"

What better method to reinforce Jesus's love than to bring in treats for the CCD children? That's the Italian way, ya know!

I still wrangle with confession. In fact, as I grew older, and the numbing effect of confession receded; it became a comical event. My friend and I would go to confession together. The Cathedral and its silent and somber tone gave us the giggles. We tried sitting at opposite sides of the church to avoid laughing. Glancing toward one another is all it took. We ended up running out of the church before the priest could hear or see us.

"Thou shalt not laugh in church!" Confess it!

My stance on disclosing my sins to a fallible priest has not wavered. I'd rather speak directly to Blessed Mother. She is my mentor. I am devoted to her. She has blessed me with her spiritual guidance, in all trials and tribulations. My devotion to her is broadcast inside and outside of my home. I could open a shop; selling rosary beads that I have acquired from every part of the globe. I have relics of Mother Mary in my bedroom. In front of my home is a three-foot statue of Mary; as protector of my domicile. She has been an unwavering companion my entire life.

The angel, Gabriel, never came to greet me with sacred tidings. My two daughters, Paulette and Michelle, were birthed the natural way—detachable penis and all. Bloody Mary stayed away nine months at a time. The mystery is that Dusty also had two girls. Their names are Maryann and Donna. The four girls were born only three months and six months apart. How's that for unscheduled due dates?

The conception of the Christ-child and His birth, however, is not one of jest. The awe and beauty surrounding Christmas is a renewal of promise that lends hope, faith, love, and salvation from our Savior. Christmas is an unfailing, breathtaking, humbling, and inspiring wonder.

Little Rosemarie remembers Christmas as a sacred and simple tradition. A more materialistic flavor has taken place over the Christmas season. In my era, Santa Claus took a backseat to the true meaning of the holiday. Practical gifts were given over material gifts; such as toy soldiers, trains, dolls, and games. One toy was a sufficient gift. Dusty and I were thrilled to receive a ragdoll or coloring books. Pajamas, slippers, and sweaters were a more desirable and practicable selection.

The anticipation of family and friends gathering together to celebrate was invigorating. Christmas Eve was an endless array of fish in every form. Fried eel, smelts, scallops, shrimp, and spaghetti aglio overfilled plates. Antipastos and rice pies and cannolis were plentiful. All appetites were satiated with mounds of food, conversation, and Italian bread in all its glory!

The house was brimming with aromas of fish, anisette, a licorice liquor, coffee-perking, and eggnog-sipping. A toast to good health and prosperity. The positive expectation for the Epiphany and new year were hopeful! Musical artists, like Perry Como and Bing Crosby, sang Christmas songs from a record player with the volume set to low. The radio was also a method to listen to holiday songs and artists. Gossip windows were closed in observance of the holiday!

It always seemed to snow in time for Christmas. What a delight. My brother, Michael, was in charge of purchasing the Christmas tree every season. He would inspect every pine tree to ensure there were no hidden bare spots. He purposely purchased a tree that was too tall for our ceiling. He enjoyed listening to my father swear at him, and sweat, while he attempted to cut the tree to size. As the buyer of the tree; he also made himself the chief decorator.

Every strand of tinsel had to be positioned on the appropriate branch. My sister and I were allowed to string popcorn and make paper chains of green and red construction paper. Dusty and I never understood why each morning, we would see missing popcorn from strands of the tree. Limp gaps of string replaced plump kernels. Was it a little elf or a critter consuming the treats? Cotton balls served as dollops of snow.

The Christmas lights were awkward and heavy; weighing down the boughs of the tree. The angel positioned on the treetop was the most important figure of all. She safeguarded the manger; placed in the center of the tree-skirt. Neatly wrapped gifts of pretty paper and ribbon were arranged on each side of the manger. Stockings overflowing with candy and confections hung from the fireplace mantle.

A popular toy my sister and I received one year, was a walking doll. We couldn't believe our eyes. Walking dolls had just become popular! They were a wish of every girl that Christmas. The arms and legs moved. The doll would walk with you when you held her hand. She had long, thick braids. My doll had brown hair, and my sister's doll had blonde hair. Her face was porcelain with blue eyes, red cheeks, and rosy lips. She was beautiful. Her dress was of gingham material. White socks and shoes completed her outfit. The doll was the epitome of perfection. We were elated!

On Christmas day, the family dressed in their best attire to honor the birth of Jesus at Sunday mass. Another round of scrumptious foods; turkey with the trimmings, ham, lasagna, desserts—awaiting ravenous consumption. In those days, folks measured ingredients by eye. A pinch of salt, a dash of pepper, a sprinkle of oregano.

You actually had to sit and observe the cook to learn how to make traditional dishes. Recipes were handwritten, and ingredients were then measured by conjecture.

Adult Rosemarie craves the company of her massive family on nostalgic holidays like Christmas. My brother, Michael, passed away several years ago, on this holiday favorite.

The most precious gift I received from him, before his departure, was the same manger we kept under the tree—all those years ago. The original figurines have aged, but are still in good condition. They hold so many memories of joyful family traditions.

I am almost positive that one of his Heavenly duties is to keep the family in line. I know that he is enjoying every moment of the challenging task. *Good luck with that, Michael!*

I am so fortunate to have a husband that has been given the gift of voice. His musical career began as a choir boy. He continues to praise Jesus with his lulling tenor voice. Midnight mass on Christmas Eve is an especially holy and miraculous event. The sacredness, love, and warmth of the Christ-child embody the spirit.

The manger displayed on the altar and the trees of Christmas light lend a stillness and adored silence. The birth of a newborn King. My husband, Edward, sings "O Holy Night!"

We are reminded of what the holiday season is really about. Rejoice! The Lord has come! We worship and adore Him! We glorify Him! We praise His holy name!

My children, Paulette and Michelle, are the joys of my life. I can only hope that I did not impart too many of my dysfunctional family traits to them. "Thou shalt not indoctrinate thy children!" Confess it!

I will continue to journey the remainder of my life with the knowledge that I am protected and shielded by my loving family in Heaven. They are still guiding me. That may be viewed as a positive or negative omen. Life is a day-by-day adventure.

Instead of opening the gossip window; they have a more convenient method of communication. They can part the clouds and peek at what is going on in our lives.

"Hey! Rosaria and Mike! Do you see what your Rosemarie is doing? She made a bad decision there. A dumb move. Who taught her to think like that? Momma Mia! She needs help! You gotta talk to her in her dreams or something. Get in her head and tell her to think—use her cabasa! She's not six years old anymore. For crying out loud! There is no excuse! She is an adult now! What happened to the wisdom you taught her? Fix that kid!"

"Let me know if you get through to her. I am going to the beach to dig for periwinkles and clams. We're having spaghetti and seafood for dinner tonight. Set the table!"

Young Rosemarie has nudged me to close the window and pull down the shade. She does, however, want to offer some wisdom to you. Contrary to, and in spite of the periwinkle gossipers' opinions.

These words of wisdom will carry you through.

"There is no room for doubt. You can always pray it out! Repent, repeat, confess! Repent, repeat, confess! Redeem Yourself!" Confess it!

PRAYERS REFERENCED IN NARRATIVE

Rosemarie's Commandments are listed last!

THE TEN COMMANDMENTS

God gave Moses the Ten Commandments on Mount Sinai. They were to serve as principles of moral for mankind.

1. I am the Lord thy God, thou shalt not have strange gods before me.
2. Thou shalt not take the name of the Lord thy God in vain.
3. Remember the Sabbath.
4. Honor thy father and thy mother.
5. Thou shalt not kill.

6. Thou shalt not commit adultery.

7. Thou shalt not steal.

8. Thou shalt not bear false witness against thy neighbor.

9. Thou shalt not covet thy neighbor's wife.

10. Thou shalt not covet thy neighbor's goods.

ACT OF FAITH

O my God, I firmly believe that you are one
God in three divine persons.
Father, Son, and Holy Spirit. I believe that
your divine Son became man
and died for our sins and that he will come
again to judge the living and the
dead.

I believe these, and all the truth, which the
Holy Catholic Church teaches
because you have revealed them. Who are
eternal truth and wisdom.
Who can neither deceive nor be deceived. In
this faith I intend to live
and die. Amen.

ACT OF HOPE

O Lord God, I hope by your grace for the pardon of all my sins. And after life here to gain eternal happiness because you have promised it. Who are infinitely powerful, faithful, kind and merciful. In this hope I intend to live and die. Amen.

ACT OF LOVE

O Lord God, I love you above all things. I love my neighbor for your sake because you are the highest infinite and perfect good, worthy of all my love. In this love I intend to live and die. Amen.

THE ROSARY

The name *Rosary* signifies the crown of roses. Rosary beads are used to pray. There are ten beads to a decade of five. The full Rosary is twenty decades with four sets of five mysteries. The twenty mysteries to reflect when saying the Rosary are the Joyful, Luminous, Sorrowful, and Glorious mysteries.

THE SIGN OF THE CROSS

In the name of the Father, and of the Son, and of the Holy Spirit, Amen.

THE APOSTLES' CREED

I believe in God, the Father Almighty, Creator of Heaven and earth. I believe in Jesus Christ, his only son, Our Lord, who was conceived by the Holy Spirit, born of the Virgin Mary, suffered under Pontius Pilate, was crucified, died, and was buried. He descended into Hell. The third day, He rose again from the dead; He ascended into Heaven and sits at the right hand of God the Father Almighty. From thence he shall come to judge the living and the dead. I believe in the Holy Ghost, the holy catholic church, the communion of saints, the forgiveness of sins, the resurrection of the body, and life everlasting. Amen.

GLORY BE

Glory be to the Father, the Son, and the Holy Spirit. As it was in the beginning is now, and ever shall be. World without end. Amen.

THE LORD'S PRAYER

Our Father who art in Heaven, hallowed be Thy name. Thy kingdom come, Thy will be done on earth as it is in Heaven. Give us this day our daily bread, and forgive us our trespasses as we forgive those who trespass against us; and lead us not into temptation but deliver us from evil. Amen.

HAIL MARY

Hail Mary, full of grace, the Lord is with thee. Blessed art thou amongst women, and blessed is the fruit of thy womb, Jesus. Holy Mary, Mother of God, pray for us sinners now, and at the hour of our death. Amen.

HAIL HOLY QUEEN

Hail Holy Queen, Mother of mercy, our life, our sweetness, and our hope! To thee we cry, poor banished children of Eve, to thee do we send up our sighs, mourning and weeping in this valley of tears. Turn, then, most gracious advocate, Thine eyes of mercy toward us; and after this our exile. Show unto us the blessed fruit of Thy womb, Jesus!
O Clement, O loving, O sweet Virgin Mary.
Pray for us, O Holy Mother of God that we may be made worthy of the promises of Christ. Amen.

CONFESSION

Bless me Father, for I have sinned. It has been . . . since my last confession.
These are my sins . . .

ACT OF CONTRITION

O MY GOD, I am heartily sorry for having offended Thee, and I detest all my sins because I dread the loss of Heaven and the pains of Hell. But most of all because they offend Thee, my God, who art all good and deserving of all my love. I firmly resolve with the help of Thy grace to confess my sins and to do penance and to amend my life.

Amen.

ROSEMARIE'S COMMANDMENTS

1. Thou shalt not disobey thy grandfather.
2. Thou shalt not murder Jesus; in theory.
3. Thou shalt not worship money.
4. Thou shalt not bribe Jesus.
5. Thou shalt not befriend a demon.
6. Thou shalt not treat children like garbage.
7. Thou shalt not ogle women in bathing suits at the beach.
8. Thou shalt not steal with or without permission.
9. Thou shalt not baby the baby.
10. Thou shalt honor the brides of Jesus.
11. Thou shalt not exhibit any of the listed deviant behaviors, and then some.
12. Thou shalt not impose guilt on children.
13. Thou shalt not treat siblings the same.
14. Thou shalt not practice incorrect writing for Jesus.
15. Thou shalt not be jealous, or wish harm on thy fellow classmates.
16. Thou shalt not cram material into thy brain.

17. Thou shalt not make fun of the nuns.

18. Thou shalt not have dirty sex.

19. Thou shalt not encourage sex in thought, word, or deed.

20. Thou shalt not give thy kid the brushoff.

21. Thou shalt not tell scary sex tales.

22. Thou shalt not make love to a man.

23. Thou shalt not argue with thy Heavenly Father.

24. Thou shalt not admit thy dysfunctionality.

25. Thou shalt not laugh in church.

26. Thou shalt not indoctrinate thy children.

Little Rosemarie lived by the twenty-six commandments. She formulated a Bible for them. The cover was coated with licorice-flavored scent.

The title of the Bible: "Unfair Confessions of kids!"

Her commandment (or commanding Bible) was her companion to help her cope with the daily grind of the times. The era she was mixed into to endure her childhood. Dropped into a void by some unknown entity into an abyss of guilt and shame.

She persevered; stayed strong; gained wisdom. She managed in spite of her questionable upbringing and indoctrination of the Catholic faith; and the Unmerciful Sisters of Mercy!

Oh! And by the way, her tome is written in exaggerated, calligraphic, cursive form!

Little Rosemarie became her own savior! She chants "Good for me! Arise! I am vindicated!"

Thank you so much for purchasing this book!

Now I would really appreciate your feedback. Your input will help to make the next version even better.

Please leave a helpful REVIEW on Amazon.

I will personally read each one.

~Rosemarie

ABOUT THE AUTHOR

Rosemarie Chauvin was reared in the 50's era. Her biggest challenge was surviving the Italian/Catholic upbringing, traditions, and customs of the time. The comedic narrative addresses her childhood experiences and perceptions in a quirky, witty, sarcastic, and humorous manner.

She would like her fellow victims of the Catholic church and classmates who suffered abuse by the nuns, to read her recollections and raise their voice in united perseverance!

Rosemarie is a former New Englander who currently resides with her family in sunny Florida. Her passion is to entertain her audience and offer them a slice of life in a startling rewind mode.

Since working with kindergarten children for fourteen years; Rosemarie is now retired and able to devote more time to her passion of writing books. She has published several articles for church and newspaper publications. As well as a variety of poems and sonnets. Her first ebook is a children's book titled ***Bethany's Bike and Santa Jail!***

You can bond with "Little Rosemarie," the narrator, by purchasing the story, sitting back, and allowing the child to confess at the "gossip window!" Is your curiosity piqued? Get in touch with Rosemarie by emailing her at rosemariechauvin@gmail.com

ACKNOWLEDGMENTS

"ODE TO SELF-PUBLISHING SCHOOL"

Chandler Bolt and Sean Sumner rock the
school like no other.
Thanks for giving me the opportunity.
Now I can publish my book without fear.
Knowing that you both will be near.
You gave me all the tools to succeed.
You catered to my every need.
Chandler Bolt and Sean Sumner rock the
school like no other! Yeah!

Self-publishing school also provided me with
the best publishing mentor I could have ever
imagined. Qat Wanders' beauty reigns inside
and outside. She is so well-educated in the

field of writing and editing, and a host of other accomplishments. She is also a best-selling author and a master at her craft.

I am so grateful to you for your advice, editing, and ease of accessibility. You are a joy and pleasure to work with. Your personality is uplifting, encouraging, and infectious!

Thank you, Qat, over and over again!

To learn more about Chandler, Sean, Qat, and Self-Publishing School, please click this link to watch Chandler's FREE TRAINING to learn how you can go from blank page to published author in ninety days!

https://xe172.isrefer.com/go/sps4fta-vts/book brosinc4797

One Last Thing…

Little Rosemarie is offering a proposition to YOUR Little inner child!

She thinks it would be fun to share YOUR story. You know, an incident when you were embarrassed or misunderstood the dogma and traditions of your faith.

Listen to your younger self. The child may be eager to share a comical situation.

Did you have issues with your Italian/Catholic era? How about a different era and religious experience?

All are submissible.

Any culture or denomination are acceptable.

Come on, consider the offer. Little Rosemarie is already excited! We love laughter!

We want to give you the opportunity to have your piece reviewed for inclusion in the next book series. For more details, please email rosemariechauvin@gmail.com and put "Book Submission Details" in the subject line.

In the meantime, "Thou shalt confess thy juicy gossip!"

10187681R00084

Made in the USA
San Bernardino, CA
28 November 2018